Christmas
in the Gold Fields, 1849

The Reminiscences of

Joseph J. McCloskey & Hermann J. Sharmann

with illustrations taken from contemporary

LETTER SHEETS

PUBLISHED BY

THE CALIFORNIA HISTORICAL SOCIETY

SAN FRANCISCO

669452

DESIGNED AND PRINTED BY LAWTON KENNEDY

"*Looking Backward Sixty Years. Two Sturdy Veterans of the Golden Desert Recall Their Hardships in the Season of Peace and Goodwill.*" *Personal interviews in the San Francisco Call, December 19, 1909.*

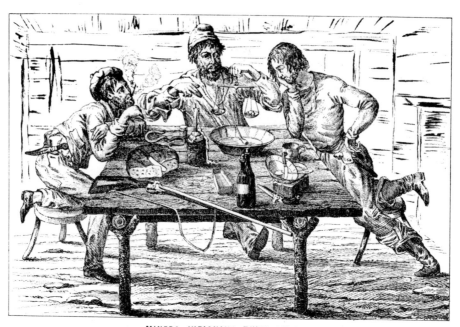

MINERS WEIGHING THEIR GOLD.

INTRODUCTION

Few are the links that remain to connect us in the celebration of our Christmas with the strange Christmas that the westward wandering pioneers celebrated in California in the gold year, 1849. The word "Forty-niner" itself is little more than a legend, a term for characters in fiction or drama these days. But in New York two men are still living who observed the day 60 years ago on the virgin soil of the new up-springing state. And they have a story to tell.

They are veterans of a notable era, these men. In the strength and hope of their youth they had a part in the struggle that gave us all our magnificent domain toward the sunset, that wrested an empire from beyond the hopeless bulwarks of desert and isolation and savagery. We know the glamor of that time and that struggle. But they have known the bitterness of it [too].

One of the men is Joseph J. McCloskey, 83 years old, dean of the actor playwrights of America, who has seen much of life and is yet active and alert and ready for much more of it. He is clerk of the city court, goes to business every day and has a limitless fund of anecdote. He was 23 years old at his '49 Christmas. The other is Hermann J. Sharmann, 71 years old. After a successful

[9]

career he has passed his large brewing business over to his sons, and he lives now, quietly, happily, at his home in Central Park South. He was 11 years old at his '49 Christmas.

The contrast between their Christmas experiences 60 years ago finds an echo in the men themselves. Mr. Sharmann is placid, dignified, heavily built, with a commanding face and an impressive manner. Mr. McCloskey is slight, volatile, smiling, with a ready tongue and expressive gestures. The one had a very sad and the other, a right merry Christmas, and it may seem that each still bears the mark upon him. Both represent the best type of Americans and are well worth knowing . . .

Mr. McCloskey was born in Greenwich Village, home of famed New Yorkers and ancient tradition. The "old Ninth Ward" he calls it, and thereby proves his birthright. When he was a youngster "Fourteenth Street was 'way out," and he remembers having had Aaron Burr, then a decrepit old man, pointed out to him on Broadway. This is his story:

WHEN the gold stories began to come in there was nothing for it but I must go west. Transportation was the great problem, and separation of the sheep from the goats was on the basis of whether a man wanted to go with reasonable comfort by sea or with unreasonable discomfort by land. Fortunately I was in a position to choose the former.

Young men with the gold fever used to gather into 'hundreds' for the trip. At one time there were three or four meetings of 'hundreds' every night at the old Ashland house. I fell in with a 'hundred' with my little stake and became one of the proud possessors of the Flavius, a full rigged ship, which we bought outright at the dock and stocked within a week.

We had an eventful voyage. At Rio we helped the Emperor of Brazil celebrate his marriage, off the Horn we froze and battered about for six weeks, in Valparaiso we got into trouble with the *vigilantes,* or mounted police, and off Juan Fernandez our crew mutinied. The St. Mary's, then a war vessel, afterward the schoolship, came to our aid, and we entered San Francisco harbor with American blue-jackets in the forecastle.

[11]

Early in December I was a full fledged placer miner at Wood's creek, a tent village which clung and gripped and slipped along the banks of a ravine below the point where the first comers had built a dam. I took up a claim on the sands, and had more money inside a week than I ever hope to see again. The population numbered short of 60, all men and all square men. The favorite conception of a California pioneer as a vagabond with a gun in each hand, a knife between his teeth and eyes roaming for a fight, was formed by writers who were never west of the Ohio. The men with whom I worked were blue shirted and rough garbed, perhaps, but they were not ruffians. They were judges, lawyers and physicians, yes, and clergymen among them.

Things were going nicely with Wood's creek when the camp turned in on the night of December 21. We were prosperous, we had plenty of provisions, and even a blanket under a tent roof is luxury in some circumstances. About midnight I awoke to find myself swimming under the tent cover, rain beating all about and the roar of a loosened cataract in my ears. The dam had burst.

I crawled up to the higher ground, abandoning my outfit, to find the rest of the camp gathered there, above the reach of the flood, but drenched and miserable. In the darkness we could hear the rushing tide below us that was sweeping over our sandbars. our flumes and our tools. It looked hopeless to me. My impulse was to leave the whole thing, to close the chapter. The prospect of perching on that bank until the water chose to fall and then laboriously restoring what we had lost did not appeal to me. I turned to two of the crowd, boys about my own age, and proposed that we push on out of it, to some other settlement or to find some of our own. They agreed and we had finished our scanty preparations by dawn.

I never learned the names of my two chums, except that one answered to Steve and the other to Mat. Steve was a red haired little crab of a chap, with a grin broader than his face, a happy, foot loose wanderer, who had left whatever home he might have known as a child and had been kicking about most of creation ever since. Mat was tall, built on the clothes-horse plan, with a face of chronic melancholy that belied his disposition. He had left his folks back in Vermont somewhere to tempt fortune in the west.

We had lost nearly everything in the flood, of course, and our commissariat was rather weak. Steve rounded up part

MAKING NOTHING.

MAKING SOMETHING.

of a side of bacon and I contributed about a pound of hard-tack. With this and a rusty frying pan we started off, heading up the creek. I can't remember that any of us had much notion of our ultimate destination. I am quite clear that none of us cared particularly We were in the golden land, there was no one to call us to account, the air was clear and bracing. And, better than all else, we were young.

When we made camp that night, some 20 miles up from Wood's creek, in a strange and untraveled section, we ate more than half our stock of food in sheer animal improvidence. Next day we lazied along without undue effort. We were a little more careful of our supplies this time, and went to sleep with a hungry spot inside us.

You must remember that during this jaunt we were keeping no count of the time. We were living each moment as it came, content with physical well being, enjoying the new country, the daily change of scene and our own good company. The first annoyance we suffered was the third night out, when we fried the last of our hardtack with the rind of the bacon.

We awoke at sunup. It was a bright morning, with the early chill still in the air, but with promise of a warm day ahead. We had thrown our blankets by a clump of bushes near the creek and Steve set about building a fire with the dead branches he could pick up. We had struck no trees for miles; the country was green and open save for our sheltering bushes. Steve was crouching over the blaze and Mat and I were stretching and watching him idly.

'What are we going to have for breakfast?' says Mat, all of a sudden. We hadn't considered that part of it. Steve, with the empty, frying pan in his hand, held it over the fire and laughed. 'Well, we've got everything but the food,' he says. 'We can pull in our belts for the rest of it.' I was ready enough to smile and pass the thing off in a reflection of his own plucky spirit, when I glanced at Mat. I never could tell when Mat was serious and when it was only his expression, but there was a deeper shade on his face.

'Good Lord, boys!' he says. 'Do you know that this is Christmas?'

Well, it was pretty tough, coming that way. I felt as if some one had pulled a prop away from under me with a jerk. We stared at each other a minute and then we all looked away again.

It was Christmas. The land was green and pleasant, but

it had lost its charm for us. Steve, who had never known much of a home, poor fellow! was as much cut up as Mat and myself. As for me, it was the first time I had ever been away from my mother at that time of year. I'm not ashamed to say that I stepped away from my companions, went around to the other side of the bushes and sat down and cried. I was pretty young.

But right when I was feeling sorriest for myself and thinking about home and how I wished I was there I began to see how selfish and short sighted I was. After all, there were three of us and it was small friendship to comrades to hide myself and mope. So after a few minutes I strolled back. Mat was sitting with his head in his hands, the picture of desolation, thinking about the farmhouse in Vermont, I suppose. Steve was trying to assume a cheerful air and making a failure of it while he fussed around the useless fire.

'Look here, boys,' I said, 'this is playing it pretty low down on each other. I'm ready to celebrate. Merry, Christmas, Steve. Merry Christmas, Mat. Here, you two kids, Santa Claus has come.'

They stared at me as if I'd lost my senses, but I hadn't. I took out of my belt two heavy little nuggets I'd been saving to send back to New York and gave one to each of them. It was a poor enough gift. Gold was a common commodity with us. They'd have appreciated a hot biscuit a lot more. But it fetched them. The downright absurdity of the idea struck them right, I guess, for I had them smiling.

Then, of course, they had to get in the game with holiday offerings. Steve dug up a broken bladed pocketknife for me and a silk handkerchief for Mat. Mat had a jasper watch charm for Steve and a little silver pencil for me. We spread out our gifts and gloated over them and laughed over them, though I guess there were tears back of the laughs.

'Youngsters don't ever eat any breakfast on Christmas morning,' says Steve; and we jumped at the suggestion and wouldn't even tighten up our belts for fear we'd break the rules. Perhaps we added to ourselves that if youngsters forget breakfast they come in pretty strong on dinner, and we hadn't much prospect for that. But we started the day right and we stuck to it. After some chaffing we took up our march and followed the creek again.

We kept up the fiction that we were satisfied and tickled to death with our presents for some hours, but under the sun we began to notice the lack of food, and conversation died

[19]

down. Along about noon we were in the doldrums again, marching side by side and saying nothing. We came to a wooded rise after a while and we began to climb it slowly, resting often and feeling pretty weak. We were stopping for breath about half way up when something happened.

Through that solitude, in the untrodden wilderness, 100 miles, as we supposed, from any living soul, there came the musical chant of voices. Sweet and true the melody filtered down to us through the trees—'*Adeste, Fideles,*' the hymn of all hymns for Christmas! We looked up, baring our heads mechanically. I don't think we would have been surprised after the first strain to see a troop of angels among the branches. I know I was quite convinced that some supernatural manifestation had been vouchsafed to us. We could see nothing, but still the voices rose and fell. I scarcely dared to move, but Steve, who was more practical, let out a whoop and dashed on up the hill. We followed him to the top and in a little open space we found our angels.

There were four of them, young men from Boston. It appeared that they had belonged to a church choir and had traveled to California together. They were in the hills prospecting and were making the most of their Christmas. They were well supplied with provisions, flour and sugar and bacon, and they welcomed us joyfully. You may be sure we were grateful.

They stayed our hunger, but announced that the big celebration would be in the evening. We were content, and during the afternoon all seven of us sat around and swapped yarns. In the evening we built a gorgeous fire, and one of the singers, who had a knack, cooked marvelous flapjacks in bacon grease. Then we had bootleg coffee, so called from its color, and the chef finally achieved his greatest triumph and our undying admiration by producing a rough sort of johnny cake, baked on a shovel.

It was a rare feast, unimpeded by dishes in the absence of any, and digested by the aid of talk and laughter. We had enough to tell each other. Every man had some tale of Christmas to add, and we exchanged all the stuff we could remember or had read that would contribute to the occasion. Toward the end some one produced a modest flask and we had a drink around to do fitting honor to our happy gathering. Perhaps a newcomer blundering into our camp might have thought us a rather questionable crowd, with our torn and stained garments, our heavy boots and our general unshorn and unkempt appearance. But if we lacked the polish, out there in the new, uncharted country, we had the will and the sentiment.

There never was a more successful Christmas dinner, and when we sat back, replenished, warm, filled with the glow of good food and kindly company, we three strangers had thankful hearts for the cheer and shelter to which we had been led on this day of days. Grouped about the fire, we all sang the old Christmas songs again and again, the eyes of each man seeking and finding in the flames familiar scenes of home far back in the east. Then when the blaze had fallen to embers and the shadows began to steal in upon us from the forest we shook hands all around, with the clasp of friends, wished each other once more a 'Merry Christmas,' and so to our blankets.

Mr. Sharmann was born in Germany and was brought by his parents to the United States before he was a year old, with his brother Jacob, four years older than himself. The family lived in Brooklyn for some time, and when the older Sharmann decided to join the army of California gold seekers there was a little daughter 4 years old. This is Mr. Sharmann's story of his '49 Christmas.

WE TOOK the overland route to the west, starting early in 1849. It took us nine months to make the trip and, young as I was at that time, the terrible sufferings and privations we endured have never been effaced from my mind.

At Independence, Mo., we left behind us the last vestige of civilization and plunged into the trackless regions of the great plains. My father was made captain of a train of 75 imigrants who banded to make this dangerous stage of the journey together. Our family had one wagon, a prairie schooner it was called, and a yoke of oxen. It was slow, difficult traveling and for weeks we plodded on and on into a world that was a brown, flat plate under an inverted blue cup.

The train broke up as we advanced, and when we had crossed the Rockies and were struggling into the terrors of the great American desert we were alone. Misfortune swept upon us when we had covered part of that hopeless stretch. Our water was nearly gone, our cattle died and packing such supplies as we could carry on our shoulders we staggered on toward the goal. My brother and myself were strong and well able to do our share, but my mother and little sister grew weaker.

Day by day we threw away our possessions to enable us to make the distance we must make or perish. Finally, after a period that has since been nothing but a haze of torture in my memory, we won the slope of the Sierras. Here we began to climb. We had made only a short distance when my sister died. We buried her where we chanced to be, on a mountain side. I have never been able to identify the spot.

December found us established on our first claim. The nearest settlement was Bidwell's Bar, though that was nothing more than two or three tents, and the nearest town was Marysville, 90 miles away. We had no neighbors, and my mother was the only woman for many miles around in that wilderness. With our depleted supplies we were in bad case. A sheet of canvas stretched on piles served us for a house. It did little but keep the full sweep of the rain from finding us. Furniture we had none, nor beds. We slept on the ground, wrapped in our ragged blankets. By day my father, my brother and myself worked at placer mining on the Upper Feather river.

My mother never recovered from the effects of the trip across the desert . . . Toward the middle of the month my father, too, fell ill. His trouble was scurvy, due to the wretched food, which was all we could procure. We had managed to get a horse and my brother rode to Marysville, where he bought some potatoes at $2 a pound and about a gill of vinegar. We scraped the potatoes and soaked the scrapings in vinegar. With this we saved my father's life.

As Christmas approached we two youngsters fell to making plans. Brought up, as all Germans are, to regard Christmas as the great fete of the year, the time for reunions and merry making and great good cheer, we could not quite forego observing it, though there was little to rejoice in. We had saved a small quantity of gold dust as our share of the mining operations and we determined to spend it in celebrating.

Two days before Christmas, my father then being somewhat better, my brother and I mounted the horse and started for Marysville, riding foremost by turns. We followed the trail down the river and reached the town worn and tired, but happy for a time in the sound of new voices, the sight of men and dwellings and the thought that we might purchase some few articles in the store. It took us a long time to make our selection. We had, I think, about $10, not enough for a gift for each one of us.

'What do you see that would make a welcome gift to the father and the mother?' my brother asked me. I looked over the few shelves of goods hopefully. There were some calicoes and some colored 'kerchiefs that I thought my mother might like but [I feared] she would never live to wear them. I saw a bright, sharp hunting knife that I wished I might get for my father, but it seemed scarcely the thing to give a sick man. It seemed to me that nothing would be so welcome to them as some delicacy that would break the monotony of the bad food, the soggy flapjacks and salt meat.

'Let us buy something good to eat,' I said, and we turned to the provisions. We hesitated over a box of sardines and some smoked herring, until it occurred to us that we wanted a still rarer and more tempting dish. Jacob reached over and picked up an object with a glaring label.

'Herman,' he cried. 'Look at this. Canned peaches! Could anything be so delicious? Let us take peaches.' I agreed and we found that the storekeeper would let us have the peaches for the sum we had brought with us. He had but one can and regarded it as the most desirable thing in his stock.

After carefully wrapping up our prize and tying it firmly to Jacob's belt we mounted our horse again and started back. When dawn was breaking on Christmas morning we reached our camp by the river.

Our parents, lying on their blankets, answered our wishes of a 'Merry Christmas,' as cheerfully as they could. We kissed each other tenderly and talked for many hours of the former happy Christmas days we had spent back in our Brooklyn home. Jacob had brought with him a branch of pine which he had plucked on our homeward journey and he set this up in the earth that formed our floor.

'It is our Christmas tree,' he said, and our good mother and father smiled through their tears. We found some bits of ribbon and cloth and all the little trinkets we had retained. With these my brother and I dressed our poor tree and we sat before it, trying to think that it was glorious, all covered with brilliant baubles, and loaded with sweets and packets of good things.

'What did you get in Marysville?' my father asked. But we only nudged each other mysteriously and would not tell. That was to be the big surprise, and the feast that should make us all believe that we were back in the pleasant land of plenty.

We set about preparing the Christmas dinner with great

A SUNDAYS AMUSEMENTS.

A DAILY PLEASURE.

secrecy and care. Jacob fried the flapjacks and made coffee. I mixed flour and water for the biscuits. We had not known salt since our arrival and we used a substitute which was commonly adopted among the forty-niners, gunpowder. It gave some little savor to the food, though I should scarcely recommend it as a condiment.

When everything was in readiness we set out an empty box between the pallets on which our parents lay. This was the table. We had two pails which served well enough for chairs for Jacob and myself. We brought in the hot meal on tin plates and arranged everything neatly where father and mother could reach without getting up. We both left the tent then and ran to where we had hidden the peaches. We opened the can with a knife and Jacob, as the elder, had the honor of carrying it in.

We came in procession, Jacob leading and bearing the peaches like a butler bringing in the wassail bowl, I following. Jacob placed the can on the box with great dignity and looked at father and mother for applause. And then we had our crushing disappointment. Neither of them could touch the delicacy nor could either taste the meal which we had arranged with so much pride. We both cried a little, but our mother comforted us and told us that we should eat the share for them. So we sat down and divided the peaches. I am afraid that most of the flapjacks and the biscuits were wasted. Our hunger and the rare treat before us made us forget the sorrow of the futile gift and we ate until not even a trace of syrup was left inside the can.

That was our Christmas in California in '49. It was a time when we were close to bitterness and pain . . . Many happy Christmas days, I have passed since then, but always there comes a moment, when my children and my grandchildren are about me, when I remember our sad celebration under the canvas roof on the banks of the Upper Feather river.

ACKNOWLEDGMENTS

This little book was designed and printed by Lawton Kennedy. His meticulous craftsmanship and creative spirit have graced many publications of the California Historical Society, through the years.

All illustrations derive from the Society's extensive collection of lithographed "Letter Sheets" done by such well-known firms as Britton & Rey, Kuchel & Dresel, C. J. Pallard et al. The earliest date back to the Gold Rush and "surely [they were] the godparents of the illustrated postal card of today."* Lonely miners bought them for a few cents to send back home, with messages written where pictures were not. Sometimes there was a double spread of exciting scenes; sometimes no more than a vignette in a corner, leaving four empty pages of notepaper.

*"California on Stone" by Harry T. Peters (Prologue, page 11), published by Doubleday, Doran & Company, Inc., New York, 1935.

THE DREAM OF A PROSPECTING MINER.